The King's Cats

Written by
Cath Jones

Illustrated by
Leo Trinidad

Queen June was sitting on her throne playing her silver flute.

All of a sudden, there was a loud yell. "The King and his cats have come to visit!"

"Oh no!" Queen June said. "Not the cats!"

"Sister, we have come to stay for three weeks!" said the King.

The King had lots and lots of cats. He kept them with him all the time.

The cats slept in all the royal beds.

In the morning they yowled and poked Queen June until she woke up.

Then they clawed her bed.

"Feed me!" said the cats.

"Fuss me!" they said.

A whirl of cats ran from room to room.

Some of them chased Queen June's little dog.

"Shoo!" said the queen.

Some of the cats ran off with Queen June's hats!

"These cats need rules," said the Queen. "They are bad cats!"

"No, they are not bad," the King said. "They just like to play."

The King's cats **were** bad cats!

They ran up and down Queen June's chimneys. They dug holes in the royal gardens. They scoffed food off the royal plates.

"There's a cat on my throne," Queen June moaned. "And there's a cat in my crown! These cats are pests!"

Queen June set off to do a bit of soothing gardening.

But there were cats snoozing under the royal roses. They stuck out their claws and jumped up at the Queen.

"Ow!" she said.

The cats ran up and down all the trees and clawed the royal tree trunks. They dug up the royal flower beds too.

Queen June fled up the steps, out of the garden and along the royal tunnels.

So Queen June made some rules for the cats.

> Cat Rule Number 1:
> No cats in the royal beds.
>
> Cat Rule Number 2:
> No digging in the royal garden.

But the cats kept on sleeping in the beds and digging in the garden.

They were so rude!

Now Queen June was fed up. The cats were just too much.

She picked up her phone. "Mum! Can you rescue me from the King's cats?" she asked.

"Use the royal flute," said the Queen Mum. "Cats do not like the toot-tooting of flutes."

… and the King and all those annoying cats fled!

Queen June was so thrilled, she did a little jig.